Introduc

Travelling between Blaenau Ffestinic
through the Lledr Valley. Whether you
the soaring mountain tops, ancient forests ɛ   ⸗ ⸗ⅎ uⅼS
unique valley beckon. And the fact that the ⸗⸗⸗uʃⱱape is the setting for a
spectacular castle and ancient church, and that it is traversed by a famous
Roman road, provides an additional incentive to visit the area.

The circular walks described here range in locality from the north of
the valley, where the Lledr and Conwy rivers converge, to the south, where
the infant Lledr emerges from the mountains above Blaenau Ffestiniog. The
walks are readily accessible from the village of Dolwyddelan, while the
larger centres of Betws-y-Coed and Blaenau Ffestiniog are a short distance
away using the railway line between Llandudno and Blaenau Ffestiniog or
the A470 road. Most of them start from one of three stations on the railway
line: Pont y Pant, Dolwyddelan or Pont Rufeinig (Roman Bridge).

Any of these walks can be undertaken by a reasonably fit person, with
Walks 3, **7**, **11** to **13** and **15** being the most challenging and *requiring good
visibility when attempted*. Walking boots or strong shoes are recommended
for all of them. *Please remember that the walks pass through sheep farming
country in which dogs must be kept permanently on a lead.*

The location of each route is shown on the back cover and a summary of
the main characteristics and approximate length of each is shown on a chart.
An estimated duration is also given but it is best to allow longer in order to
linger over the many fine views and interesting places visited whilst on
the walks. Each walk has a map and description which enables the route
to be followed without further help. However, remember to take account of
weather conditions before setting out and dress accordingly, especially if
you intend to explore any of the higher routes. A weather forecast for this
area is available on **09068 232785** (charge) or at www.met-office.gov.uk.

The *Conwy Valley Rail Initiative*, which is a partnership of community
stakeholders supporting the Conwy Valley Branch Line from Llandudno
to Blaenau Ffestiniog, is pleased to be associated with this excellent pub-
lication, which will be invaluable for visitors and locals alike who enjoy
the spendour and the outdoor wonders of the Conwy and Lledr Valleys.

BWLCH Y MAEN

DESCRIPTION This delightful 4-mile stroll takes you to a point high above the Lledr Valley from where there are good views of Gwydir Forest and the Carneddau. On the return you descend to the valley floor and walk down to the confluence of the Wybrnant and Lledr rivers. You then follow the Afon Lledr back to the starting point. Allow two hours.

START Parking space at the junction near the Lledr bridge on the road from the Lledr Valley to Tŷ Mawr (SH798539).

DIRECTIONS *From Betws-y-Coed:* From its junction with the A5 just south of Betws-y-Coed take the A470 towards Blaenau Ffestiniog. After a short distance the A470 bends sharply right, crosses the Afon Conwy and then bends sharply left. Take the next minor road on the LEFT at a point (very soon) where the main road bears right. Cross a bridge and go ahead to a junction where the road to the right is signposted Tŷ Mawr. Between the two tarmac roads is the wide entrance to a forestry track signposted 'Bwlch y Maen and Fedw Deg only'. Park on the right of the entrance. *From Blaenau Ffestiniog:* Take the A470 north in the direction of Conwy. Pass through Dolwyddelan and, after about 4 miles, pass under a railway viaduct. Soon after this take the minor road on the RIGHT in the middle of a left-hand curve in the main road. Cross a bridge and go ahead to a junction where the road to the right is signposted Tŷ Mawr. Between the two tarmac roads at the junction is the wide entrance to a forestry track signposted 'Bwlch y Maen and Fedw Deg only'. Park on the right of the entrance.

I Follow the forestry track gently uphill, soon to emerge from the trees. There are good views here of Moel Siabod to the south and of the crags on the opposite side of the Lledr Valley at this point. The track twists and turns, and then goes into the forest again. When the track divides, take the LEFT-hand fork and continue uphill to another junction. Here bear RIGHT, pass a turning circle and go through a metal gate (or to the left of it if locked) to reach another clearing. The clearing enables you to see the lie of the land with the steep-sided Wybrnant Valley (see **Walks 2** and **12**) falling to the Lledr Valley from the left. You can also see, below you the magnificent railway viaduct over the Lledr. The track briefly re-enters the forest before emerging. Pass a field gate on the left before reaching a metal gate and stile on the right. *There are more good views to be had from this point, with the Carneddau dominating the skyline across the Lledr Valley.*

2 Go RIGHT over the stile here and follow a track downhill across a field. The track bears right alongside a stream which is on its left. Ignore a track going left and continue down on the main track until you reach a metal gate. Go through and ahead until just before the padlocked gate into the building of Bwlch y Maen when you should bear half RIGHT. Follow this track past a manure heap and then go RIGHT downhill by a barn. Bear LEFT as the track takes you below the barn and past another gateway into Bwlch y Maen. Go alongside the garden wall of the house to arrive at the grassy clearing, and magnificent viewpoint, in front of it.

3 Follow the track which descends from right to left in front of Bwlch y Maen, soon to re-enter the forest. Soon the track bears sharply RIGHT and goes down alongside a fence. Ignore a footpath sign and stile over this, and continue downhill on the main track, which has a wall on its right and the fence, then a wall, on its left. Cross a stile over a fence at right-angles to the track and walk further downhill until you reach a forestry track. Cross the track and, passing a yellow marker, follow the wide path beyond it across a stream and down to a tarmac road.

4 Walk over the road, ahead and then turn sharp LEFT to go alongside a wall downhill. Soon you come to a metal gate and stile. Go through/over, cross a stream and continue downhill on a track which has a steep drop down to the Afon Lledr on its right. Pass some fencing and descend to the river bank ahead. *This is a delightful spot for a picnic. You are surrounded by rushing water and lush vegetation, and just around the corner*

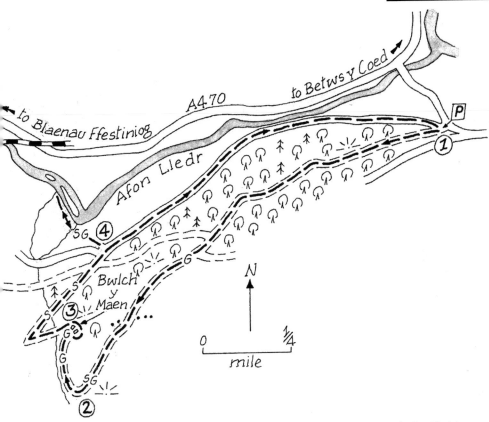

is the junction of the Lledr and Wybrnant rivers. The Lledr is famed as a salmon river, and up the valley from this point (see **Walk 4)** there is a fisherman's path on the west bank of the river which uses a series of ricketty ladders and gangways to reach the Lledr's deepest and least accessible pools. Return to the tarmac road and turn LEFT onto it. Then follow the road back along the valley to your starting point.

View over the Lledr Valley

3

WALK 2

TY MAWR FROM PONT Y PANT

DESCRIPTION A 6-mile walk through forest to the idyllic spot, high in the Wybrnant Valley, which is the setting for the historic house of Tŷ Mawr (*open from 12-5pm, 20 March to 30 September, excepting Mondays, Tuesdays and Wednesdays*). The return takes you alongside the Afon Lledr on sections of an old road up the valley. Allow three hours.

START Parking space on the railway bridge just north of Pont y Pant station (SH754537).

DIRECTIONS *From Betws-y-Coed:* From its junction with the A5 just south of Betws-y-Coed take the A470 towards Blaenau Ffestiniog. About a mile after passing under a railway viaduct, take the minor road on the LEFT signposted Pont y Pant station and Plas Hall Hotel. Cross the river, bear RIGHT at the hotel entrance and park on the railway bridge a short distance further on. *From Blaenau Ffestiniog:* Take the A470 north in the direction of Conwy. Pass through Dolwyddelan and, after about 2 miles, take the minor road on the RIGHT signposted Pont y Pant station and Plas Hall Hotel. Cross the river, bear RIGHT at the hotel entrance and park on the railway bridge a short distance further on.

1 Go ahead over the bridge then turn LEFT up the track signposted as a footpath. Bear RIGHT at a junction and follow the track past a house to the large settlement of Bwlch Bach. Continue on the track, ignoring a footpath sign pointing right, bear LEFT at a junction and remain on the track ignoring another footpath sign. Soon the track goes downhill, with views of the Lledr Valley below, to meet a track on the left as it goes alongside the railway line. You will return to this point later.

2 Continue ahead as the track goes uphill below rocky crags high above you. Take the unmarked footpath off to the RIGHT (a continuation of a path coming up from the left) just before a passing space on the left of the track. The path is well made and goes uphill, soon alongside a wall on the left, to

pass a giant slab of rock before going down to a wooden gate. Go through and turn RIGHT, by the buildings of Cyfyng, onto the metalled road beyond. Go uphill steeply past a sign for Tŷ Mawr and alongside a wall on the left. *There are good views of the Lledr Valley from here and, as you pass some rocky outcrops on the right, of waterfalls on the Afon Wybrnant just over the wall.* Soon go through two metal gates, the second by a stream, past a house on the right, then through a third gate and past Pwll y Gâth. Go through a wooden gate and across the river to reach Tŷ Mawr. *Tŷ Mawr was the birthplace of Bishop William Morgan who was the first to translate the Bible into Welsh. His translation was published in 1588 and so pre-dated the King James Bible by over 20 years. The house is owned by the National Trust and has been restored to its 16th Century appearance. An exhibition on the life and work of Morgan is provided.*

3 Return along the road to Cyfyng. Then go back through the forest to the point reached at the end of section **1**. Take the forest trail going down (now to your RIGHT) alongside the railway line. Go to the RIGHT under the line when you see a bridge and then turn sharp LEFT next to a wooden post with a green arrow. Follow the well-made path alongside a wall, beyond which is the railway line, on the left. Soon pass another

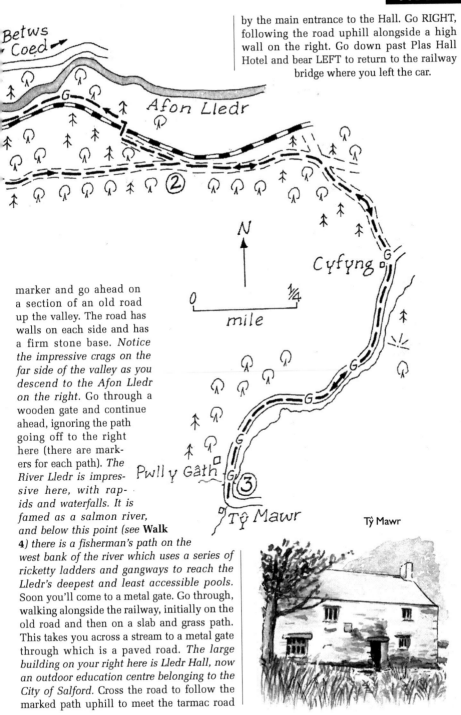

Betws
Coed

Afon Lledr

② N

Cyfyng

Pwll y Gâth

③

Tŷ Mawr

Tŷ Mawr

0 ¼
mile

by the main entrance to the Hall. Go RIGHT, following the road uphill alongside a high wall on the right. Go down past Plas Hall Hotel and bear LEFT to return to the railway bridge where you left the car.

marker and go ahead on a section of an old road up the valley. The road has walls on each side and has a firm stone base. *Notice the impressive crags on the far side of the valley as you descend to the Afon Lledr on the right.* Go through a wooden gate and continue ahead, ignoring the path going off to the right here (there are markers for each path). *The River Lledr is impressive here, with rapids and waterfalls. It is famed as a salmon river, and below this point (see* **Walk 4**) *there is a fisherman's path on the west bank of the river which uses a series of ricketty ladders and gangways to reach the Lledr's deepest and least accessible pools.* Soon you'll come to a metal gate. Go through, walking alongside the railway, initially on the old road and then on a slab and grass path. This takes you across a stream to a metal gate through which is a paved road. *The large building on your right here is Lledr Hall, now an outdoor education centre belonging to the City of Salford.* Cross the road to follow the marked path uphill to meet the tarmac road

WALK 3

UNDER MOEL SIABOD

DESCRIPTION A wild walk which crosses the high moorland to the east of Moel Siabod and provides some spectacular view of this mountain and of the Carnedd range to the north of it. Allow three hours for this 8-mile walk.

START Parking space on the railway bridge just north of Pont y Pant station (SH754537).

DIRECTIONS *From Betws-y-Coed:* From its junction with the A5 just south of Betws-y-Coed take the A470 towards Blaenau Ffestiniog. About a mile after passing under a railway viaduct, take the minor road on the LEFT signposted Pont y Pant station and Plas Hall Hotel. Cross the river, bear RIGHT at the hotel entrance and park on the railway bridge a short distance further on. *From Blaenau Ffestiniog:* Take the A470 north in the direction of Conwy. Pass through Dolwyddelan and, after about 2 miles, take the minor road on the RIGHT signposted Pont y Pant station and Plas Hall Hotel. Cross the river, bear RIGHT at the hotel entrance and park on the railway bridge a short distance further on.

I Walk back to the A470 road. Cross it and go through a wooden gate to join a grassy path. Follow this, ignoring stone steps on the left. Cross a stile by a metal gate then continue until you reach a wall with a stone stile next to a footpath sign. Cross the wall, go LEFT onto the road beyond, then RIGHT at a junction. Go over a cattle grid and follow this road up to a house. Go through a gateway and turn LEFT to follow a track to mine workings and buildings. *This is the Rhiwgoch slate quarry, which was opened in the 1860s. The remains of its two mills and powder house can still be seen. The quarry closed in 1908.*

2 When the track divides turn RIGHT, to go uphill through mine workings and alongside a corrugated iron building on the left. Go through a gateway on the track and, soon, turn LEFT through a metal gate just above the building and go half-LEFT across a field.

Keep fairly close to the fence on your left where there some path markers. Walk uphill passing a spoil-heap on the left and then go LEFT and over a stile. Continue gently uphill on a path, passing a marker, until you reach a track at right-angles. Go RIGHT by a marker onto this track (there is a sign for Betws-y-Coed and Capel Curig at this point)

3 Soon go over a stile to the side of a metal gate and continue on the track passing more markers. When the track divides bear LEFT at a footpath sign. After the next sign the track becomes fainter but bear RIGHT here, making for another marker. *You are now entering a magnificent moorland wilderness which is dominated, to the west, by the heights of Moel Siabod.* Although the path you are following is often faint it is well marked. You are strongly advised not to leave one marker until you have sight of the next one. Soon, bear LEFT at a marker and head for a metal gate. Cross the stile here and bear LEFT alongside a rocky knoll, walking until you reach a wooden bridge. Cross the stile beyond this and find your way across boggy ground to a low marker about 100m away, slightly to the RIGHT. Bear half-RIGHT to another marker and continue between a low hill on the left and high ground to the right. *There is a good view of the Carneddau ahead of you here.* The path makes for some trees ahead. Ignore a path at right-angles and go slightly LEFT downhill at a marker by a wall. Soon you meet a track at right-angles.

4 Go LEFT onto this track and follow it, crossing a stile by a gate. At a junction of tracks, where a footpath sign points ahead, go LEFT, passing a yellow marker and crossing a stream to go uphill. Ignore a subsidiary track going left and continue ahead, crossing a stile alongside a metal gate. Soon, when you meet another track at right-angles, turn LEFT, passing an 'open access' notice. Soon, go over a stile by a metal gate and then through another gate at the forest edge. Ignore tracks on the right and then go LEFT at a signpost indicating 'Moel Siabod' to the right. Go LEFT here and follow the main track for about 1½ miles. Turn LEFT at a footpath sign near a metal gate.

5 Cross a stream and walk through the trees, passing a lake. Turn LEFT at a marker, then go RIGHT across a stile and LEFT. Soon the path reaches some ruins, where there is a marker. Go RIGHT here, keeping LEFT where the path divides. Soon, go through a wall, cross a stream and then walk downhill to a stile. Go across the field beyond then cross another stile and turn LEFT, then RIGHT onto a path marked 'Pont y Pant'. Retrace your steps from here to the starting point.

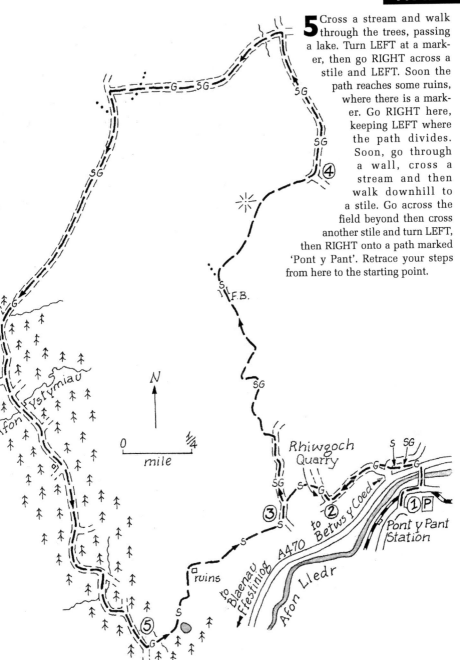

N

0 — ¼
mile

Afon Ystymiau

F.B.

Rhiwgoch Quarry

Pont y Pant Station

to Betws y Coed

A470

to Blaenau Ffestiniog

Afon Lledr

ruins

WALK 4

SARN HELEN AND THE LOWER LLEDR VALLEY

DESCRIPTION This 4½-mile walk takes you along the course of a Roman road into the forest high above the Lledr Valley on the west. You then descend to the valley bottom, where you cross the river and follow it past some of its most dramatic rapids back to your starting point. Allow three hours.

START Parking space on the railway bridge just north of Pont y Pant station (SH754537).

DIRECTIONS *From Betws-y-Coed:* From its junction with the A5 just south of Betws-y-Coed take the A470 towards Blaenau Ffestiniog. About a mile after passing under a railway viaduct, take the minor road on the LEFT signposted Pont y Pant station and Plas Hall Hotel. Cross the river, bear RIGHT at the hotel entrance and park on the railway bridge a short distance further on. *From Blaenau Ffestiniog:* Take the A470 north in the direction of Conwy. Pass through Dolwyddelan and, after about 2 miles, take the minor road on the RIGHT signposted Pont y Pant station and Plas Hall Hotel. Cross the river, bear RIGHT at the hotel entrance and park on the railway bridge a short distance further on.

1 Walk back to the A470 road. Cross it and go through a wooden gate to join a grassy path. Follow this, ignoring stone steps on the left. Cross a stile by a metal gate then continue until you reach a wall with a stone stile next to a footpath sign. Cross the wall, go RIGHT onto the road beyond, then walk uphill until you reach a point where the road divides, with the right turn marked Rhiwgoch and the left Fron Goch. Continue ahead here, going through a metal gate next to a stile and uphill on the track beyond. *You are now following Sarn Helen, the Roman road which led from the settlement at Tomen y Mur, north of Trawsfynydd, to the fort at Caer Llugwy, near Capel Curig. Some believe the road was named after Elen, the daughter of a Celtic chieftain, who married a Roman*

warrior. Soon you come to another metal gate and stile with an 'open access' marker on it. There is a good view from here south to the upper Lledr Valley, Moel Dyrnogydd (see **Walk 19**) *and Crimea Pass (see* **Walk 20**) *which the A470 road traverses on its way to Blaenau Ffestiniog. The track twists and turns as it climbs and then levels off. After* a time the track reaches a metal gate at the edge of Gwydir Forest. Go through and continue through the trees until you arrive at a forest track at right-angles.

2 Go sharply RIGHT onto this track and follow it through the forest. Soon bear RIGHT at a junction and go uphill. *When you emerge from the trees just after this point you can see the distinctive outline of Moel Siabod (see* **Walk 7**) *over to the right.* The track descends gently and through a cleared patch of trees. Soon after this bear RIGHT at a junction and follow the track downhill. The track passes to the left of boulders. Continue down on it, ignoring a track which soon comes in on the left, until you reach another junction. Go RIGHT here, then uphill and to the right before arriving at a turning circle on the left opposite a rocky outcrop. Keep to the left of the turning circle to find a yellow marker (very easy to miss). Go LEFT here and steeply downhill, following blue markers. Soon, the path descends wooden steps to the A470 road by a footpath sign.

3 Cross the road, go LEFT then RIGHT through a gate in the wall and down some steps. Walk along underneath the wall over rough ground until you reach a road coming down from the A470. (As an alternative follow the main road and go RIGHT at the junction). Turn RIGHT and follow the road downhill, over the Lledr and through a metal gate. Ignore a track going left, go uphill and turn RIGHT just before Tan Aeldroch Farm at a signpost for Dolwyddelan.

4 Ignore a metal gate on the left and go ahead on the path down to the river. Soon cross a stile, go through a gap in a wall and uphill through trees. Bear RIGHT at a marker to go alongside the river. *The Lledr is at its most dramatic here as it sweeps*

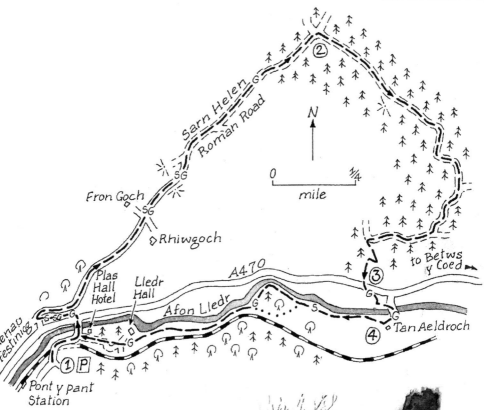

through a chasm. The old fishermens' hut and path, with its ricketty ladders and walkways, can be seen winding its way along the cliffs on the opposite bank of the river. Pass the remains of a metal bridge then go LEFT at a footpath sign and up to a wooden gate with yellow markers. Turn RIGHT and soon you'll come to a metal gate. Go through, walking alongside the railway on a path which eventually takes you across a stream to a metal gate and road next to Lledr Hall. Cross the road and go uphill, turning RIGHT to follow a road uphill alongside a high wall. Go past Plas Hall Hotel and bear LEFT to return to the starting point.

Fisherman's path above the Lledr

DOLWYDDELAN VILLAGE

DESCRIPTION This walk offers a fascinating introduction to Dolwyddelan and its picturesque situation at the confluence of the Cwm Penamnen and Lledr rivers. After visiting the site of the original ford across the Afon Lledr you walk up to a point above the valley which provides a bird's eye view of the village and its surroundings. Then you visit the splendid ruins of Dolwyddelan Castle before returning to the village to see the ancient church. Allow two hours for this 3-mile walk.

START Parking space at Dolwyddelan station (SH738522).

DIRECTIONS *From Betws-y-Coed:* From its junction with the A5 just south of Betws-y-Coed take the A470 towards Blaenau Ffestiniog. At the crossroads just past Y Gwydyr pub in the centre of Dolwyddelan, take the road on the LEFT signposted Dolwyddelan station. Pass the church on the right, then go over the river and bear LEFT just before the railway bridge. Park by the station on the RIGHT. *From Blaenau Ffestiniog:* Take the A470 north in the direction of Conwy. At the crossroads just before Y Gwydyr pub in the centre of Dolwyddelan, take the road on the RIGHT signposted Dolwyddelan station. Pass the church on the right, then go over the river and bear LEFT just before the railway bridge. Park by the station on the RIGHT.

1 Return past the school and go RIGHT over the bridge across the Afon Lledr and then along the road towards the centre of the village. After a short distance go RIGHT through a metal kissing-gate opposite the church and alongside a footpath sign. Follow the well-maintained footpath across the river meadows until you go uphill and reach a second kissing-gate. *If you look down to the river on your right at this point you will see the remains of the original ford across the Lledr. Sarn Helen, the Roman road from Caer Llugwy, near Capel Curig, to Tomen y Mur, in the hills above Trawsfynydd, leads to this spot. Said to be named after the*

wife of a Roman emperor, the road climbed from here into the Penamnen Valley above Dolwyddelan (see **Walks 9** *and* **10**). *No doubt the existence of the ford helped create the settlement that was ultimately to become Dolwyddelan.* Go through the gate, cross the main road (the A470) beyond and turn RIGHT. Go LEFT just past the house named Gwynfryn and steeply uphill on a tarmac road marked 'Unsuitable for motors'. Bear RIGHT when the road bears sharply left, going up on an unsurfaced track past some ruined cottages on the left and a fence on the right. When you reach a T-junction, where the track is briefly surfaced in tarmac, turn LEFT and follow this track to a cattle-grid and metal gate. A short distance after this the track reaches a wooden seat from where the view over Dolwyddelan is extensive. *The Crimea pass over which the A470 goes to Blaenau Ffestiniog can be seen to the south (see* **Walk 20**), *as can the castle, while the steep-sided Penamnen Valley stretches into the hills to the south-east. The crags on the left of the valley are those of Carreg Alltrem (see* **Walk 8**). *The mountain summit above Carreg Alltrem is Ro Wen (see* **Walk 13**) *and the ridge to the right of the valley is that of Moel Penamnen (see* **Walk 11**).

2 Follow the track downhill from the seat towards a wooden gate and house. Turn LEFT just before the gate, then immediately RIGHT, as indicated by the markers, and continue downhill alongside the fence below the house. Cross a stile over a wall and then go half-LEFT down a field towards a metal gate, stile and footpath sign. Cross the stile and turn RIGHT onto the metalled road beyond, going downhill to a junction. Keep RIGHT here, passing a house named Breffni on the right. Continue through this upper section of the village until you reach the main A470 road. Turn RIGHT at this junction and follow the footpath on the right of the road away from Dolwyddelan village. After about ½-mile, just before a monument on the left of the road, take a gated track going uphill on the RIGHT, passing farm-buildings before you reach the castle. *Tickets for the castle, which is open daily except over Christmas and New Year, cost £2, or £1.50 for over-60s*

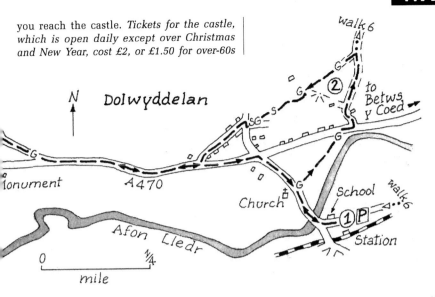

and children. *The main part of Dolwyddelan Castle was built early in the 13th Century. Maredudd ap Ieuan ap Robert, of the Wynn Family of Gwydir, subsequently lived in the castle and it was he that built Dolwyddelan Church which you will visit later.*

3 Return to the main road and follow it back into Dolwyddelan, keeping on the left-hand footpath as you enter the village to avoid having to walk on the carriageway. Turn RIGHT at the crossroads in the village centre and walk past the Spar grocery store on the right-hand side of the road leading to the sta-tion. After a short distance you will come to Dolwyddelan Church. *This tiny, well-kept church dates back to about 1500 when Maredudd ap Ieuan built it on a site some distance to the north of the original, wooden church. It contains a memorial to Maredudd, and members of the Wynn family, which was erected during the 17th Century.* Turn RIGHT after leaving the church and follow the road until you reach the bridge over the Afon Lledr. Go LEFT just before the bridge and go past the village school to reach the station car-park.

Looking across Dolwyddelan to Cwm Penamnen

11

PONT Y PANT

DESCRIPTION After crossing the Afon Lledr in Dolwyddelan you walk up into the low hills bordering the river valley. From here you descend to Rhiwgoch quarry, one of the most important slate workings in the area, before crossing the Lledr once more to reach Pont y Pant station. The return walk follows the railway line back to Dolwyddelan and is mostly alongside the river which, here, is in a particularly lush setting. Allow 2½ hours for this 4 mile walk.

START Parking space at Dolwyddelan station (SH738522).

DIRECTIONS *From Betws-y-Coed:* From its junction with the A5 just south of Betws-y-Coed take the A470 towards Blaenau Ffestiniog. At the crossroads just past Y Gwydyr pub in the centre of Dolwyddelan, take the road on the LEFT signposted Dolwyddelan station. Pass the church on the right, then go over the river and bear LEFT just before the railway bridge. Park by the station on the RIGHT. *From Blaenau Ffestiniog:* Take the A470 north in the direction of Conwy. At the crossroads just before Y Gwydyr pub in the centre of Dolwyddelan, take the road on the RIGHT signposted Dolwyddelan station. Pass the church on the right, then go over the river and bear LEFT just before the railway bridge. Park by the station on the RIGHT.

1 Return along the right-hand side of the road to the church and turn RIGHT, through a metal kissing-gate, following a footpath to a gate by the main A470 road. *If you look down to the river on your right at this point you will see the remains of the original ford across the Lledr.* Go through, cross the road and bear RIGHT, walking a short distance to pass the house named Gwynfryn before going LEFT uphill, taking the road marked 'Unsuitable for motors'. Soon, at a left-hand bend, go RIGHT uphill following an unmetalled track with a fence on the right. At the next junction, turn RIGHT, then at a forestry track go LEFT then immediately RIGHT by a footpath sign. Cross a stream and follow the path over several bridges through the trees, passing a lake on the right. Turn LEFT at a white marker to go alongside the forest, then cross a stile over the fence on the RIGHT and go LEFT past several markers. The path goes downhill before climbing to the ruins of a barn, just beyond which there is a marker pointing RIGHT.

2 Go behind the ruins, keeping LEFT where the path divides. Soon, go through a wall and below a rocky outcrop to pass several markers close together. Cross a stream and go downhill to reach a stile. Go over and across a field, passing two markers and crossing another stile to reach a track from the farm on your right. Turn LEFT and, after a short distance, RIGHT onto a downhill path marked 'Pont y Pant'. Soon cross a stile then bear RIGHT, making for a metal gate near to some buildings. Go through and turn RIGHT onto the track beyond it, going downhill past the buildings and through the quarry workings. *This is the Rhiwgoch slate quarry, which was opened in the 1860s. The remains of its two mills and powder house can still be seen. The quarry closed in 1908.*

3 Turn LEFT when the track divides, going downhill initially and then following the track to a house. Turn RIGHT and go through a gateway just before the house. Then follow the winding tarmac road down, crossing a cattle-grid before you reach a road junction. Turn LEFT here and then very soon go RIGHT at a footpath sign, crossing a wall on stone steps. Go ahead, making for a metal gate and stile, and then following a grassy path beneath the house above to the left. Ignore stone steps to the right and go through a wooden gate to reach the A470 road. Cross this and join the minor road marked Pont y Pant station which crosses over the Afon Lledr. Pass the Plas Hall Hotel on the left and bear RIGHT, ignoring a footpath sign to the left. Cross the railway as you continue along the road, ignoring a track going left, to reach Pont y Pant station. *Pont y Pant is a halt on the railway line from Llandudno Junction to Blaenau Ffestiniog. There are six or so trains in each direction on weekdays and it would be possible to shorten the walk by catching a northbound train back to Dolwyddelan.*

4 Go past the station, following the road to wooden and metal gates where the tarmac surface ends. Go through and uphill on the track before descending to a metal gate and stile by the railway line. After these walk downhill, RIGHT under the line and then immediately LEFT. The track is next to the Afon Lledr now and passes two houses on the left before reaching a metal gate. Go through and follow a tarmac road, ignor-

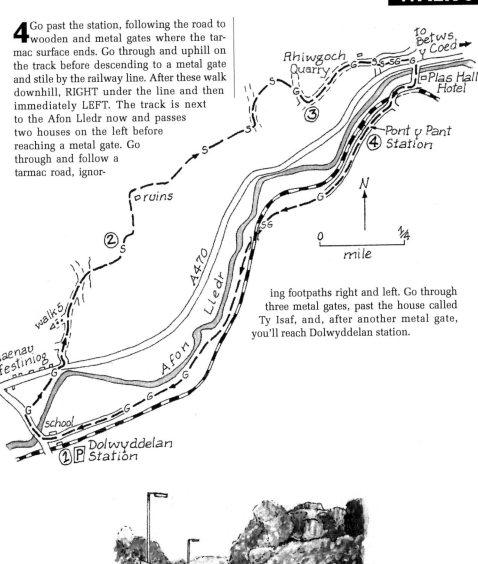

ing footpaths right and left. Go through three metal gates, past the house called Ty Isaf, and, after another metal gate, you'll reach Dolwyddelan station.

Southbound train approaching Dolwyddelan

13

MOEL SIABOD

DESCRIPTION A 10-mile walk during which you visit two spectacular locations, Llyn y Foel which nestles under the ramparts of Moel Siabod, and the triangular summit of this famous mountain with its wide-ranging views of Snowdonia. The descent takes you along the ridge of Siabod, over its dramatic rock formations, and then past the impressive ruins of Rhos Quarry. Allow 6½ hours.

START Parking space at Dolwyddelan station (SH738522).

DIRECTIONS *From Betws-y-Coed:* From its junction with the A5 just south of Betws-y-Coed take the A470 towards Blaenau Ffestiniog. At the crossroads just past Y Gwydyr pub in the centre of Dolwyddelan, take the road on the LEFT signposted Dolwyddelan station. Pass the church on the right, then go over the river and bear LEFT just before the railway bridge. Park by the station on the RIGHT. *From Blaenau Ffestiniog:* Take the A470 north in the direction of Conwy. At the crossroads just before Y Gwydyr pub in the centre of Dolwyddelan, take the road on the RIGHT signposted Dolwyddelan station. Pass the church on the right, then go over the river and bear LEFT just before the railway bridge. Park by the station on the RIGHT.

1 Return past the school and go RIGHT across the Afon Lledr. After a short distance go RIGHT through a metal kissing-gate. Cross the river meadows to reach a second kissing-gate. Go through, cross the main road beyond and turn RIGHT. Go LEFT just past Gwynfryn and uphill on a tarmac road. Bear RIGHT when the road bears left, going up an unsurfaced track past ruined cottages. At a T-junction, turn RIGHT and continue uphill alongside a wall. When you reach a forestry track turn LEFT onto this, ignoring a footpath sign opposite. Soon you emerge from the forest and gain your first glimpse of Moel Siabod. The walk takes you up to the summit along the ridge on the left. Ignore tracks to left and right and follow the main track over a river. Again, ignore tracks to left and right,

cross a river and stay on the main track until you reach a fork signposted Moel Siabod left, Capel Curig right.

2 Go LEFT here, ignoring subsidary turns as the track climbs and does a zig-zag. *Pause here for a good view south to the Crimea Pass on the A470 road (see* **Walk 20***).* When the track ends cross a wooden bridge to follow a path uphill to a stile at the edge of the forest. Once over, follow the path uphill on the right of a stream. Climb steeply up a gully to reach a dam at the edge of Llyn y Foel. *This is a spot at which to linger since the cliffs of Siabod are suddenly revealed towering above the lake, which was once famed for the quality of its trout and is eight acres in area.*

3 Go LEFT along the edge of Llyn y Foel, following an obvious path which, beyond the lake, takes you half-RIGHT up onto the rocky ridge leading up to the summit of Siabod. A steep climb, which involves some scrambling, follows before you emerge from the rocks. Keep LEFT to reach the triangulation station which is perched on the summit pyramid. *The view from Moel Siabod is extensive, with the Snowdon and Glyder ranges dominant to the west. Dolwyddelan lies below, tucked into the valley between Siabod and Ro-Wen (see* **Walk 13***). Northwards is Allt Fawr with the Rhinog mountain chain beyond.*

4 Go down from the summit making for the rocky north-eastern end of the ridge of Siabod. Once you reach the rocks scramble over a series of minor peaks as the ridge narrows. Keep to the left before the last peak so as to avoid a steep drop to the right. *There are some good views from the ridge during this section, with the Mymbyr Valley left and the Lledr Valley right.* Follow the ridge down, keeping to the left over grassy slopes, to go RIGHT onto a path which has skirted the ridge top. At a wall coming from the right go half-RIGHT, making for the end-post of a fence. Go LEFT of this, cross a stile and go LEFT onto a mine track. Soon, after a metal gate and stile, take a grassy track to the RIGHT, passing a ruin on the left and making

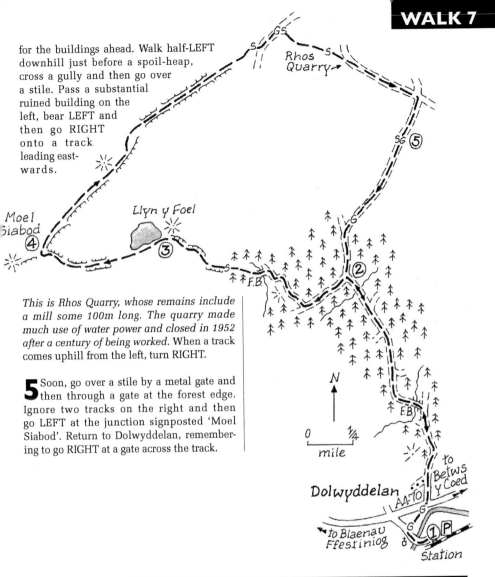

for the buildings ahead. Walk half-LEFT downhill just before a spoil-heap, cross a gully and then go over a stile. Pass a substantial ruined building on the left, bear LEFT and then go RIGHT onto a track leading eastwards.

This is Rhos Quarry, whose remains include a mill some 100m long. The quarry made much use of water power and closed in 1952 after a century of being worked. When a track comes uphill from the left, turn RIGHT.

5 Soon, go over a stile by a metal gate and then through a gate at the forest edge. Ignore two tracks on the right and then go LEFT at the junction signposted 'Moel Siabod'. Return to Dolwyddelan, remembering to go RIGHT at a gate across the track.

About the author, Michael Burnett

Michael is a musician who has written articles and presented radio programmes about Welsh traditional music. He is also the author of a Kittiwake guide to walks around the Rhinog mountains in Meirionnydd. Michael's links to Wales go back to his teenage years when he regularly stayed with friends near Maentwrog and to the 1970s when he lived with his wife, Paula, and their two young children at Blaen Myherin, a remote farmhouse above Devil's Bridge which has now, sadly, become a ruin. Today Michael and Paula share an old farmhouse near the northern Rhinog ridge.

WALK 8

CARREG ALLTREM

DESCRIPTION This pleasant 2½-mile stroll takes you into the Penamnen Valley with its magnificent cliffs and fast-flowing river. On the return you pass Tŷ Penamnen, an important historic site. Allow 1½ hours.

START Parking space at Dolwyddelan station (SH738522).

DIRECTIONS *From Betws-y-Coed:* From its junction with the A5 just south of Betws-y-Coed take the A470 towards Blaenau Ffestiniog. At the crossroads just past Y Gwydyr pub in the centre of Dolwyddelan, take the road on the LEFT signposted Dolwyddelan station. Pass the church on the right, then go over the river and bear LEFT just before the railway bridge. Park by the station on the RIGHT. *From Blaenau Ffestiniog:* Take the A470 north in the direction of Conwy. At the crossroads just before Y Gwydyr pub in the centre of Dolwyddelan, take the road on the RIGHT signposted Dolwyddelan station. Pass the church on the right, then go over the river and bear LEFT just before the railway bridge. Park by the station on the RIGHT.

1 Go LEFT over the railway bridge and then LEFT again. Take the second on the RIGHT, a gated forestry track. Go through to the left of the wooden gate and follow the track uphill through the trees. *After about a mile the sheer cliffs of Carreg Alltrem (High-looking Rock) come into view ahead. These cliffs are popular amongst rock climbers.* Soon the track divides, with a footpath sign indicating right.

2 For now, ignore the footpath sign and go LEFT, following this track uphill to the cliffs past a second track going off left. *There is a good view of Carreg Alltrem from the track directly below the cliffs and, if you continue a short distance past them, the head of the Penamnen Valley comes into view.*

3 Return to the junction with the footpath sign and turn LEFT to go downhill to another junction. Go RIGHT here and cross the Afon Cwm Penamnen on a wooden bridge. Go uphill to the road ahead. *This is a beautiful spot, next to the river, and the provision of tables makes it an ideal picnic site.* Go RIGHT onto the road and follow it the short distance to the ruins of Tŷ Penamnen, *Maredudd ap Ieuan's house. Maredudd was a tenant of Dolwyddelan Castle (see **Walks 5 & 16**). Tŷ Penamnen is presently being excavated and a notice giving information about it is provided.*

4 Continue along the road and pass through a metal gate. *If you look down to the RIGHT from here you will see the remains of a dam across Afon Cwm Penamnen. As you continue downhill there are good views of rapids and of a waterfall on this tumultuous river.* Soon Dolwyddelan comes into sight, with the ridge of Moel Siabod beyond it. After another metal gate you enter the village, going downhill with houses initially on the right. Ignore turnings off the road which soon ascends between walls to a railway bridge. Go LEFT over the bridge, then RIGHT to return to Dolwyddelan station car-park.

WALK 9

TY'N Y CWM

DESCRIPTION A delightful walk which takes you to the head of the steep-sided Penamnen Valley before you return past the remote settlement of Ty'n y Cwm and the precipitous Maesgwm waterfall. Allow 2½ hours for this 5-mile walk.

START See **Walk 8**

DIRECTIONS See **Walk 8**

For section **1** of this walk follow section **1** of **Walk 8**.

2 Take the RIGHT fork, as indicated by the footpath sign, and walk downhill to a junction of tracks. Keep LEFT here and follow this track uphill until it emerges from the trees. *There's a good view of the head of the Penamnen Valley from here, with the end of the Moel Penamnen ridge above the trees* *on the far right. Above you on the left are the steep slopes of Ro Wen (see* **Walk 13***).* The track now descends and reaches a four-way junction just after crossing a stream and at the point where the trees begin again. Turn RIGHT here and walk downhill on a firm, but grass-covered, track which crosses the Afon Cwm Penamnen and a tributary just before reaching a junction next to a footpath sign. Turn RIGHT here and go through two small wooden gates as you pass Ty'n y Cwm on the left. *This remote settlement is situated below the magnificent Maesgwm waterfall. It was once at the centre of mining activity as you'll notice from the spoil-heap to the south of the house.*

3 Follow the road leading away from the house, passing a ruin and grass track into trees on the left. Go sharp LEFT onto a track going uphill opposite a telegraph pole and very soon RIGHT to join a track going uphill. After about half a mile turn RIGHT onto a path going downhill next to a marker. *Before descending take the time to admire the view, this time down the valley towards Carreg Alltrem and Dolwyddelan.* Follow the marked path down to join the road again, going LEFT next to the empty settlement of Tan y Bwlch. Pass the entrance to Gwyndy Newydd on the right and follow the road until you reach Ty Penamnen (see **Walk 8**).

F or section **4** of this walk follow section **4** of **Walk 8**.

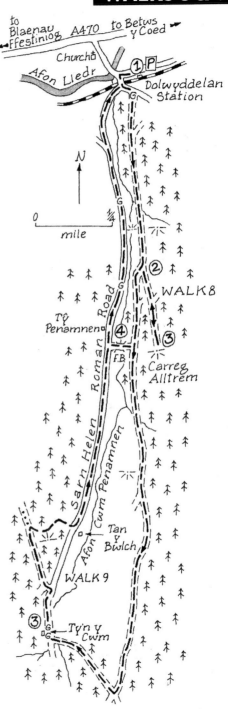

Carreg Alltrem

17

PEN Y BENAR

DESCRIPTION From Dolwyddelan you walk into the steep-sided Penamnen Valley passing the ruins of the house inhabited during the 15th Century by Maredudd ab Ieuan. You then climb up through the forest on the west of the valley to the spectacular viewpoint of Pen y Benar from where descend to the Lledr Valley near Roman Bridge. Then it's a delightful stroll along the valley floor back to the starting point. Allow 3 hours for this 5-mile walk.

START Parking space at Dolwyddelan station (SH738522).

DIRECTIONS *From Betws-y-Coed:* From its junction with the A5 just south of Betws-y-Coed take the A470 towards Blaenau Ffestiniog. At the crossroads just past Y Gwydyr pub in the centre of Dolwyddelan, take the road on the LEFT signposted Dolwyddelan station. Pass the church on the right, then go over the river and bear LEFT just before the railway bridge. Park by the station on the RIGHT. *From Blaenau Ffestiniog:* Take the A470 north in the direction of Conwy. At the crossroads just before Y Gwydyr pub in the centre of Dolwyddelan, take the road on the RIGHT signposted Dolwyddelan station. Pass the church on the right, then go over the river and bear LEFT just before the railway bridge. Park by the station on the RIGHT.

I Walk back, turning LEFT over the railway bridge and then RIGHT, following the road uphill between houses (ignore minor roads going right). After a turning space continue ahead, then through a metal gate. *You get a good view of rapids and a waterfall on the Afon Cwm Penamnen as you climb and, to the left ahead, you'll see the sheer cliffs of Carreg Alltrem (see* **Walk 8***).* Soon pass through another metal gate which is directly above a ruined dam on the river. *Now you can see to the head of the valley with the upper slopes of Ro Wen (see* **Walk 13***) above the forestry on the left of it. After a few minutes you reach the ruins of Tŷ Penamnen, Maredudd ap Ieuan's house, most of which are on the right of the road (see* **Walk 8***).*

Continue ahead on the road, to reach a parking space on the left.

2 Ignore the track going to the left, signposted 'Pont Carreg Alltrem', and continue along the valley. *The road is thought to follow the line of Sarn Helen, the Roman road from Caer Llugwy, near Capel Curig, to Tomen y Mur, the fort near Trawsfynydd.* Soon you reach a junction. Bear RIGHT and continue walking until you reach a house (Tan y Bwlch) on the left of the road.

3 Turn RIGHT by the footpath sign here and follow the path up the hillside past yellow markers to reach a forestry track. Cross the track, go through a ditch and then walk up through the trees. The path is clearly marked but sometimes wet and in a gully. Bear RIGHT at a junction of paths and continue uphill, following the path round a sharp left-hand bend to reach the forest edge. Cross the stile here and walk a short distance uphill, crossing a low, grass-covered wall. Bear RIGHT and make for the summit of Pen y Benar, going through a metal gate on the way. *The isolated position of Pen y Benar makes it an excellent viewpoint. This is dominated by Moel Siabod, across the Lledr Valley, and by the Snowdon range to the west.*

4 Go back through the gate, turn RIGHT and follow the fence downhill for a short distance. Watch for a line of stones over to the LEFT and make for these before bearing RIGHT to join the path down from the stile you crossed earlier. This is well marked and takes you to a gate and stile. Beyond this the path goes alongside a stream and joins a track coming in from the left before reaching a metal gate by an enclosure. Follow the marked track downhill to a wooden gate and stile. *There are good views from here of the upper Lledr Valley and directly ahead you can see Dolwyddelan Castle (see* **Walks 5 & 16***).* Go through two metal gates and then ahead on the track, ignoring markers indicating a path going left, to reach Bertheos Farm. Go through two metal gates, passing the farm buildings, and then ahead, ignoring a left turn in the track, to a third gate.

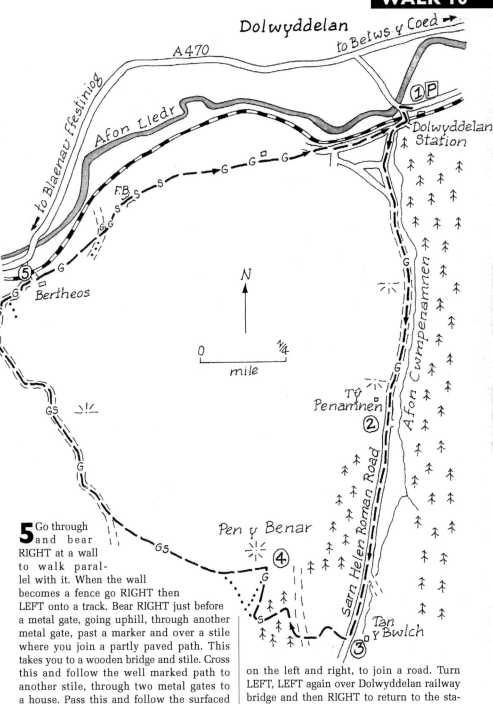

Dolwyddelan

to Betws y Coed →

A470

to Blaenau Ffestiniog

Afon Lledr

① P

Dolwyddelan
Station

F.B.

N

0   ¼
mile

⑤

Bertheos

Afon Cwmpenamnen

Sarn Helen Roman Road

To
Penamnen

②

Pen y Benar

④

5 Go through and bear RIGHT at a wall to walk parallel with it. When the wall becomes a fence go RIGHT then LEFT onto a track. Bear RIGHT just before a metal gate, going uphill, through another metal gate, past a marker and over a stile where you join a partly paved path. This takes you to a wooden bridge and stile. Cross this and follow the well marked path to another stile, through two metal gates to a house. Pass this and follow the surfaced track through another gate, ignoring tracks

Tan
y Bwlch

③

on the left and right, to join a road. Turn LEFT, LEFT again over Dolwyddelan railway bridge and then RIGHT to return to the station car-park.

19

MOEL PENAMNEN

DESCRIPTION This 8½-mile walk takes you through the forest above Dolwyddelan into the Penamnen Valley. You climb out of the valley and cross wild moorland to reach the summit of Moel Penamnen, with its dramatic south-facing crags. The descent follows an old track back down into the Penamnen Valley where you pass the excavated ruin of the house once inhabited by Maredudd ab Ieuan. Allow 5 hours.

START Parking space at Dolwyddelan station (SH738522).

DIRECTIONS *From Betws-y-Coed:* From its junction with the A5 just south of Betws-y-Coed take the A470 towards Blaenau Ffestiniog. At the crossroads just past Y Gwydyr pub in the centre of Dolwyddelan, take the road on the LEFT signposted Dolwyddelan station. Pass the church on the right, then go over the river and bear LEFT just before the railway bridge. Park by the station on the RIGHT. *From Blaenau Ffestiniog:* Take the A470 north in the direction of Conwy. At the crossroads just before Y Gwydyr pub in the centre of Dolwyddelan, take the road on the RIGHT signposted Dolwyddelan station. Pass the church on the right, then go over the river and bear LEFT just before the railway bridge. Park by the station on the RIGHT.

I Walk past the school, turn LEFT over the railway bridge and then go LEFT. Take the second entrance on the RIGHT, a gated forestry track. Go to the left of the wooden gate and follow the track uphill. *After about a mile the cliffs of Carreg Alltrem come into view ahead on the left (see* **Walk 8***).* At a junction go RIGHT by a marker and downhill. Ignore a right turn and go uphill until the track emerges from the trees. *There's a good view of the head of the Penamnen Valley from here. Soon you'll see Ty'n y Cwm, the settlement at the end of valley, also on the right and above this, the magnificent Maesgwm waterfall.* The track now descends and reaches a four-way junction at the point where the trees begin again.

2 Turn LEFT here and pass a marker as the track goes uphill with trees on the right. Ignore a track on the left and then immediately fork LEFT at another junction, following the marked track up to a track at right-angles. Cross this and take the marked grassy path going uphill directly opposite. The path winds up through the trees to a stile over the forestry fence. *This path follows the route of the Roman road, Sarn Helen, which leads to Tomen y Mur, the fort near Trawsfynydd.* Cross the stile and go RIGHT alongside the fence, through bog and then uphill, crossing another stile. Then go uphill alongside the fence until this turns right. *Look to the left here and you will see the Penmachno Valley, with its massive slate quarries. Sarn Helen continues ahead (south) from here.*

3 Go RIGHT and through a metal gate. Continue ahead towards the summit of Moel Penamnen. Bear slightly LEFT away from the forest, keeping on the grassy ridge and making for a right-angle in the fence ahead. Pass two ponds on the left as you follow a faint track which leads you alongside the fence past two stiles. Ignore these, as you go towards Penamnen through a boggy patch. After this walk half-LEFT away from the fence which now goes steeply uphill. Continue uphill between the main ridge (on your right) and a rocky hillock. Go half-RIGHT after the hillock to reach the main ridge of Penamnen. Turn LEFT and walk to the mountain top, keeping close to the left of the ridge. *Keep to the left of the two summits for the best views of their dramatic southern precipices and, once at the top, admire the wide-ranging view of mountains, from Arenig in the east to the Moelwynion in the west, and lakes.*

4 Before leaving, look along the north ridge of Penamnen and note a solitary post on a high point slightly to the RIGHT of it. Follow the faint path down from the top and walk northwards along the ridge, over some grassy knolls and keeping the post in sight. When the post disappears behind the last knoll keep to the LEFT, following the path to a stile. Cross and go half-RIGHT uphill to reach the wooden post. Here join a track leading downhill towards the Penamnen Valley. The track is marked with posts and, at the edge of the forest, turn LEFT and follow the track and forestry fence down to a metal gate. Beyond, turn RIGHT, following a marked path over a stile into the forest and downhill. The path crosses a forestry road and leads downhill to a footpath sign by a road and house (Tan y Bwlch).

5 Turn LEFT and follow the road past Gwyndy Newydd and the ruins of Tŷ Penamnen (see **Walk 8**). Go through two metal gates to reach Dolwyddelan. Ignore turnings off the road in the village. Go LEFT over the railway bridge, then RIGHT to the station car-park.

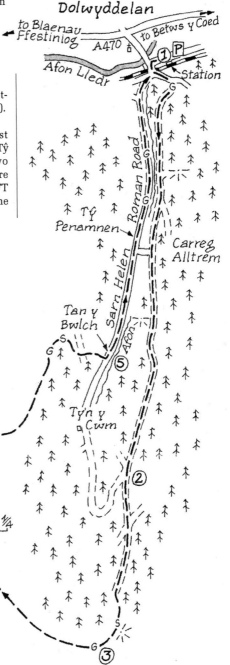

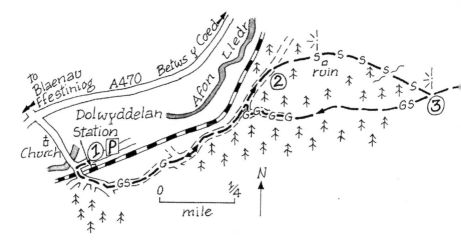

WALK 12

TY MAWR FROM DOLWYDDELAN

DESCRIPTION A fascinating 5-mile walk which takes you over the hills above Dolwyddelan to the ancient house of Tŷ Mawr, set in the picturesque Wybrynant Valley. *Tŷ Mawr is owned by the National Trust and is open from 12-5pm on Thursdays to Sundays from 20 March to 30 September.* The spectacular views of Moel Siabod make the return journey immensely rewarding. Allow four hours.

START Parking space at Dolwyddelan station (SH738522).

DIRECTIONS From Betws-y-Coed: From its junction with the A5 just south of Betws-y-Coed take the A470 towards Blaenau Ffestiniog. At the crossroads just past Y Gwydyr pub in the centre of Dolwyddelan, take the road on the LEFT signposted Dolwyddelan station. Pass the church on the right, then go over the river and bear LEFT just before the railway bridge. Park by the station on the RIGHT. From Blaenau Ffestiniog: Take the A470 north in the direction of Conwy. At the crossroads just before Y Gwydyr pub in the centre of Dolwyddelan, take the road on the RIGHT signposted Dolwyddelan station. Pass the church on the right, then go over the river and bear LEFT just before the railway bridge. Park by the station on the RIGHT.

1 Walk past the school, turn LEFT over the railway bridge and then go LEFT, continuing uphill between houses. Bear LEFT at the junction just past Glandwr and go ahead on an unsurfaced track to a metal gate and stile. Continue on the main track, ignoring right and left turns, past spoil-heaps and through another metal gate into forestry. Follow the track past a turning circle and a marked track on the left, and then uphill to a yellow marker on a post up to the RIGHT.

2 Go up to this marker, immediately bear half-LEFT by a second marker and follow a path through undergrowth, checking for an initial red mark on a tree, followed by another yellow marker, and making for a stream ahead. Cross this and bear slightly LEFT away from it, following the faint path uphill to pass another marker. Then go slightly RIGHT and uphill near the stream. Watch out for the next marker (a post with faint red paint on it) which is up to the LEFT, away from the stream. Pass this and bear RIGHT, making for a yellow marker and some ruins. *This is a good viewpoint from where you can look back over Dolwyddelan towards Cribau (see* **Walk 15***) and the Snowdon range.* Cross the stile by the ruin and walk uphill past it to a marker. Then continue uphill, making for the edge of the forest above you slightly to the RIGHT. Go through a gap in an old, grass-covered wall, cross the stile at the forest corner and continue uphill between the

22

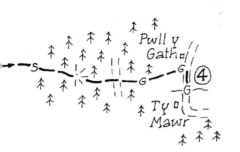

as indicated by a marker. *It is from here that you get your first glimpse of Tŷ Mawr below.* The path goes through a wall and meets another, less well-used forestry track. Turn RIGHT, then immediately LEFT where there is a sign for Tŷ Mawr, and descend, going through a gate and between walls. Just before you reach a house (Pwll y Gâth) go through a wooden gate on the RIGHT and downhill. Then turn RIGHT onto a tarmac road, going through a wooden gate to reach Tŷ Mawr.

4 Return the way you came until you reach the rocky knoll above the forest in the Lledr Valley (see section **2**). *There are glorious views of Moel Siabod (see **Walk 7**) as you cross the watershed and descend to this point.* Continue on the well-defined path you joined at the knoll, following it down to a stile and fenced-off gate into the forest next to a metal hut. Go over and pass markers as you follow the path down through the trees, crossing several streams on the way. After about a mile keep LEFT of a marker, following the path down to a rickety gate at the edge of the trees. The path continues down a field to another gateway, partly fenced off. Go through, following a track which bears LEFT and goes through another gateway. The track is now stony and goes down through a gateway to the forestry track from Dolwyddelan you followed earlier. Turn LEFT and retrace your steps to the car-park.

trees and a fence. At a marker the path bears slightly RIGHT but continues uphill to reach a stile. Cross this and bear half-RIGHT across boggy ground to a marker and another stile. Go over, back into the trees, going LEFT up a gully, then half-RIGHT to a stile next to open country. From here walk directly uphill, on the right of a stream, making for a rock and heather-covered knoll and passing a small group of conifers. Go RIGHT of the knoll and then LEFT onto a well-used path.

3 Keep to this path as it climbs to the watershed, passing a white marker, and then descends to a stile next to forestry. Once over descend into the Wybyrnant Valley. Cross a forestry track and continue downhill

Distant view of Snowdon from the ruins above the Lledr Valley

23

RO WEN

DESCRIPTION This 8-mile walk takes you up the beautiful Penamnen Valley to the summit of the mountain which dominates it to the east. The views of Snowdonia from Ro Wen are magnificent and the walk concludes with an easy stroll down a well-made track from which the picturesque setting of the village of Dolwyddelan can be seen to best advantage. Allow 4 hours.

START Parking space at Dolwyddelan station (SH738522).

DIRECTIONS *From Betws-y-Coed:* From its junction with the A5 just south of Betws-y-Coed take the A470 towards Blaenau Ffestiniog. At the crossroads just past Y Gwydyr pub in the centre of Dolwyddelan, take the road on the LEFT signposted Dolwyddelan station. Pass the church on the right, then go over the river and bear LEFT just before the railway bridge. Park by the station on the RIGHT. *From Blaenau Ffestiniog:* Take the A470 north in the direction of Conwy. At the crossroads just before Y Gwydyr pub in the centre of Dolwyddelan, take the road on the RIGHT signposted Dolwyddelan station. Pass the church on the right, then go over the river and bear LEFT just before the railway bridge. Park by the station on the RIGHT.

1 Walk LEFT over the railway bridge and then RIGHT, following the road uphill (ignore minor roads going right). After a turning space continue, going through two metal gates, the second above a ruined dam on the river. *You get a good view of rapids on the Afon Cwm Penamnen as you climb and, to the left ahead, are the sheer cliffs of Carreg Alltrem (see* **Walk 8***). From the second gate you can see the upper slopes of Ro Wen above the forestry on the left of the valley.* Soon you reach the ruins of Ty Penamnen, Maredudd ap Ieuan's house (see **Walk 8**), and then a parking space on the left.

2 Ignore the track going left, signposted 'Pont Carreg Alltrem', and continue along the valley. *The road is thought to follow the line of Sarn Helen, the Roman road from* Caer Llugwy, near Capel Curig, to Tomen y Mur, near Trawsfynydd. Soon you reach the entrance to Gwyndy Newydd on the left. Bear RIGHT and continue walking, passing Tan y Bwlch on the left. Follow the road from here to Ty'n y Cwm, at the head of the Penamnen Valley, where you go through two wooden gates. *Ty'n y Cwm is situated below the magnificent Maesgwm waterfall. It was once at the centre of mining activity as you'll notice from the spoil-heap to the south.* After the house go LEFT at a footpath sign, following a track across the Afon Cwm Penamnen and uphill through forest to a four-way junction.

3 Go AHEAD here and pass a marker as the track goes uphill with trees on the right. Ignore a track on the left and then immediately fork LEFT at another junction, following the marked track up to a track at right-angles. Cross this and take the marked grassy path going uphill opposite. The path winds up through the trees to a stile over the forestry fence. Cross the stile and go LEFT.

4 Go uphill parallel with the fence, soon passing a clearing in the forest on the left. *There is a good view of Moel Siabod (see* **Walk 7***) from here over to the left.* The path climbs a rocky ridge and becomes indistinct. Continue walking near the fence, going through a fence at right-angles by a broken-down stile. *The summit of Ro Wen is now ahead of you to the right and you can see the length of the Penamnen Valley down to Dolwyddelan on your left.* The path becomes clearer as it goes uphill away from the forest fence. Soon a fence appears to the right. Keep to the left of this and go ahead when it turns to the right, making for some small trees in the distance above the forest itself. Descend to a stream bridged with railway sleepers near the original forest fence. Then go uphill, through a broken down fence and past the small trees. Leave the forest fence when it bears left, aiming for the ridge of Ro Wen and crossing a stile before bearing RIGHT to join the ridge. Follow the path up alongside fence-posts, dropping down briefly before climbing to the summit shelter. *The view from here ranges from Snowdon in the* *west to the Arenig peaks in the east, with the Carneddau dominating the skyline to the north-west.*

5 Follow the wall westwards from the summit to join a well-made track initially going north. The track passes through three gates before going alongside a river and trees on the left to reach a third gate. It then zig-zags steeply down to the edge of Dolwyddelan where there is a gate and stile. After this turn LEFT onto a track at right-angles, go through another gate (with stile) and follow the track downhill, ignoring right and left turns. Bear RIGHT to join a tarmac road and pass a row of houses on the left. Bear RIGHT over the railway bridge and then go RIGHT again to reach your starting point.

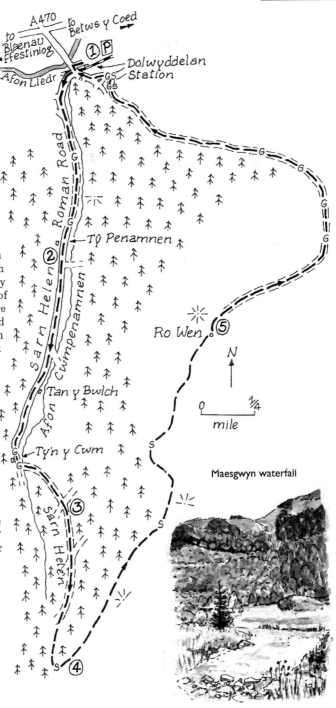

to Blaenau Ffestiniog

A470

to Betws y Coed

① P

Dolwyddelan Station

Afon Lledr

Roman Road

Tŷ Penamnen

②

Sarn Helen

Afon Cwmpenamnen

Ro. Wen ⑤

N

0   ¼   mile

Tan y Bwlch

Tŷ'n y Cwm

③

Sarn Helen

Maesgwyn waterfall

④

25

WALK 14
ACROSS THE LLEDR

DESCRIPTION This 2-mile walk takes you north from Dolwyddelan alongside the Afon Lledr which you cross on an old footbridge. You then climb gently up into the western foothills of the Lledr Valley to reach a viewpoint offering spectacular views of the Dolwyddelan area before descending to the village centre. Allow 1½ hours.

START Parking space at Dolwyddelan station (SH738522).

DIRECTIONS *From Betws-y-Coed:* From its junction with the A5 just south of Betws-y-Coed take the A470 towards Blaenau Ffestiniog. At the crossroads just past Y Gwydyr pub in the centre of Dolwyddelan, take the road on the LEFT signposted Dolwyddelan station. Pass the church on the right, then go over the river and bear LEFT just before the railway bridge. Park by the station on the RIGHT. *From Blaenau Ffestiniog:* Take the A470 north in the direction of Conwy. At the crossroads just before Y Gwydyr pub in the centre of Dolwyddelan, take the road on the RIGHT signposted Dolwyddelan station. Pass the church on the right, then go over the river and bear LEFT just before the railway bridge. Park by the station on the RIGHT.

1 Turn RIGHT at the car-park entrance opposite Dolwyddelan primary school and follow the tarmac road through a metal gate. Pass the house called Ty Isaf and go through three metal gates before reaching a point at which there are signs indicating footpaths going right and left. Go LEFT here and cross the Lledr on the stone footbridge. *Note how carefully the bridge was constructed, with several spans supported on rock pillars on each side of the water-course so as to allow for the flow of flood water. Older inhabitants of the Lledr Valley tell of how, half a century ago, the bridge was used by children walking to school from west of the river.*

2 Follow the path until you reach a kissing gate alongside the main (A470) road. Go through and turn LEFT, then immediately RIGHT, crossing the road and taking an initially tarmac-surfaced forestry track next to a footpath sign. The track begins to climb, passing some mine workings and the house named Bwlch. Follow the track as it twists and turns uphill, under some electricity wires and past a gated right-turn which leads up to a television mast. *The track is clear of trees on the left by now and there are some pleasing views from here of Dolwyddelan and the upper Lledr Valley.* Ignore a track going down to a gate on the left and continue on the main track until you reach a metal gate across it.

3 Go LEFT just past the gate, following a track gently downhill opposite a footpath sign on the right. Go through a wall and bear RIGHT at a junction where another track goes steeply down on the left. Cross a cattle-grid next to a metal gate and go uphill through grass to a seat on the right of the track. *Pause at this viewpoint for it offers wide-ranging views. Below is the village of Dolwyddelan and beyond it, to the south, you can see the steep-sided Penamnen Valley (see* **Walks 8** *and* **9**) *with the ridge of Ro Wen (see* **Walk 13**) *towering above it on the left. Looking ahead along the line of the track the A470 road can be seen ascending the Crimea Pass and there is a good view of the upper Lledr Valley and Dolwyddelan Castle (see* **Walks 5 & 16**).

4 Follow the track downhill from the seat towards a wooden gate and house. Turn LEFT just before the gate, then immediately RIGHT, as indicated by the markers, and continue downhill alongside the fence below the house. Cross a stile over a wall and then go half-LEFT down a field towards a metal gate, stile and footpath sign. Cross the stile and turn RIGHT onto the metalled road beyond, going downhill to a junction. Go LEFT here, walking downhill to the crossroads in the centre of Dolwyddelan. *This attractive village is reputed to be named after an Irish missionary, Gwyddelan, who arrived*

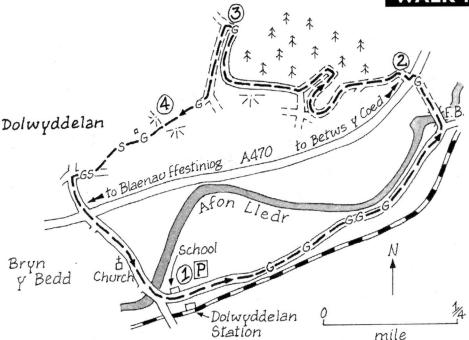

Dolwyddelan

Bryn
y Bedd   Church   School

①P

Afon Lledr

N

Dolwyddelan
Station

0   ¼
mile

here in about AD600. He built a wooden chapel near Bryn y Bedd, a hill some 100 yards to the south of the present church. Subsequently, Dolwyddelan developed as an important staging post on packhorse trails from Beddgelert and the west, Betws-y-Coed and the north, Penmachno and the east, and Ffestiniog and the south. Cross the main road here and walk past the Spar grocery store on the right-hand side of the road leading to the station. After a short distance you will come to Dolwyddelan Church. This tiny, well-kept church was built by Maredudd ap Ieuan and dates back to about 1500. It contains a memorial to Maredudd, and members of the Wynn family, which was erected during the 17th Century. Turn RIGHT after leaving the church and follow the road until you reach the bridge over the Afon Lledr. Go LEFT just before the bridge and go past the village school to reach the station car-park.

Footbridge over the Lledr

27

Y CRIBAU

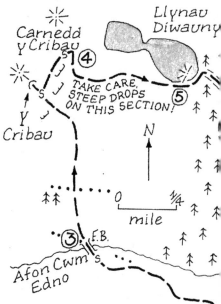

DESCRIPTION This 8-mile walk takes you across the Afon Lledr and follows an ancient trail into the hills from the old farmhouse of Coed Mawr. Leaving the trail you climb the rocky ridge of Y Cribau for an outstanding view of the Snowdon horseshoe. On the return you pass the twin lakes of Diwaunydd which nestle picturesquely beneath the flank of Moel Siabod. Allow six hours.

START Parking space at Pont Rufeinig (Roman Bridge) station (SH713514).

DIRECTIONS *From Betws-y-Coed:* From its junction with the A5 just south of Betws-y-Coed take the A470 towards Blaenau Ffestiniog. Pass through Dolwyddelan and, about a mile beyond the village, take the minor road on the RIGHT signposted Roman Bridge station. Park by the station on the RIGHT. *From Blaenau Ffestiniog:* Take the A470 north in the direction of Conwy. The road climbs over the Crimea Pass and descends steeply into the Lledr Valley. Near the bottom of the descent, soon after a three-lane stretch of road, take the minor road on the LEFT signposted Roman Bridge station. Park by the station on the RIGHT.

1 Follow the road RIGHT to a junction. Go LEFT here to a farmhouse, through a gateway and turn RIGHT. Go through a metal gate, then RIGHT through another metal gate and over a railway bridge. Go LEFT to a bridge over a stream and then sharp LEFT. Here go RIGHT off the track to cross a stream and a stile. *There is a good view of Moel Siabod to the right from here. Facing you are the remains of Coed Mawr slate quarry.* Cross the River Lledr on a wooden bridge. Then turn sharp LEFT, walking towards two marker posts. Turn RIGHT by the second, going uphill, and then LEFT at the fence. Follow the fence RIGHT (look for the marker), then go LEFT, making for a house. Go through a metal gate, cross a bridge and reach a road.

2 Turn LEFT and immediately take the RIGHT fork, signposted Coed Mawr. At the farm, go through a metal gate and then

RIGHT onto the track signposted Nant Gwynant. Follow this RIGHT after crossing a stream, and go through a metal gate. *Soon you see Y Cribau ridge, with a pointed summit midway along and a rocky nose at the right-hand end.* Pass a solitary tree to reach a gate. There are superb views here of the Snowdon range ahead and, left of it, of Yr Aran. Ignore a track going left by a mine building and descend to a stile.

3 Cross the stile and bridge over the Afon Cwm Edno then bear half-LEFT past a marker. Keep RIGHT of the stream (ignoring a path off to the right) as you pass a tree plantation to meet a path at right-angles. Ignore the markers, and go uphill alongside the stream towards the pointed ridge summit ahead. Cross the stream, going half-LEFT to a rocky outcrop, and up to the ridge past a line of rocks in a grassy gully. Turn RIGHT on the ridge to go behind the pointed summit. Then go half-LEFT to the pyramid-shaped main (eastern) summit of Y Cribau. Cross a stile to reach the western summit. *The view of the Snowdon Horseshoe is spectacular from here.* Return to the stile and turn LEFT to follow the fence, past a tarn, to Carnedd y Cribau. Ignore a first stile then cross a second one at the summit, which has its own tarn. *Again, the view is wonderful, with the Carneddau and Glyder ranges to the north, Siabod to the north-east, Snowdon to the west and Moel Hebog to the south.*

4 Carnedd y Cribau is surrounded by steep drops so care is needed on descent. Go back down by the fence, without crossing it. Shortly, it goes down into a boggy gully. Turn LEFT here (check for a metal fence post) down the gully. Soon this gives way to a grassy ridge with Llynau

Diwaunydd below. Bear RIGHT when the ridge drops steeply and go down into the gully below. Turn LEFT, following this down onto a steep hillside. Make for the RIGHT-hand far end of the lakes where a stream emerges. Cross this, go over a stile, and walk to the lake end. *Pause here to look back to the dramatic cliffs of Carnedd y Cribau.*

5 Go LEFT along the lake's edge, bearing RIGHT behind a ruined building to join a forestry track. Follow this, passing marker posts 13, 12 and 11 before stopping at post 10. Turn LEFT here into the forest, following a marked path which crosses another forestry track before reaching a stile at the forest edge. Cross this, and a stream, to go RIGHT uphill through wooden, then metal, gates. Then go RIGHT and LEFT down to another metal gate by a road. Turn LEFT, then RIGHT at a foot-path sign. Follow the marked path to a metal gate. Go ahead, then RIGHT to a wooden gate and footbridge. Cross a field and bear RIGHT to a ramp to a wooden gate and road. Turn RIGHT and follow this to Roman Bridge station.

Snowdon from the Cribau ridge

DOLWYDDELAN CASTLE

DESCRIPTION A fascinating walk, 3 miles long, which provides you with a dramatic first glimpse of Dolwyddelan Castle from the hill above. After encircling the castle you pass the flooded remains of a nearby mine before climbing beyond it to reach an outstanding viewpoint offering a panorama of the upper Lledr Valley and the mountains surrounding it. Allow 1½ hours (longer if visiting the castle itself).
START Parking space at Pont Rufeinig (Roman Bridge) station (SH713514).
DIRECTIONS From Betws-y-Coed: From its junction with the A5 just south of Betws-y-Coed take the A470 towards Blaenau Ffestiniog. Pass through Dolwyddelan and, about a mile beyond the village, take the minor road on the RIGHT signposted Roman Bridge station. Park by the station on the RIGHT. From Blaenau Ffestiniog: Take the A470 north in the direction of Conwy. The road climbs over the Crimea Pass and descends steeply into the Lledr Valley. Near the bottom of the descent, soon after a three-lane stretch of road, take the minor road on the LEFT signposted Roman Bridge station. Park by the station on the RIGHT.

I Follow the road RIGHT, past a junction and over bridges across the railway and Afon Lledr. Continue uphill until the road turns sharp left in the midst of farm buildings. Take the track, indicated by a footpath sign, off to the RIGHT here. Go through a metal gate and then through two further metal gates, each with a stile next to it. *Once through the third gate take a moment to savour the view of Moel Siabod (see* **Walk 7***) towering above you to the left.* Soon the track divides; keep RIGHT here, passing a footpath sign, and go through a fourth metal gate. The track, in less good condition now, continues gently uphill to another gate with a yellow marker. Go through to reach the top of the hill and catch your first glimpse of the keep of Dolwyddelan Castle. *This is a dra-*

matic moment, when you look down on your objective and realise how strategically it is situated; and how much more meaningful it is to visit such a site on foot rather than gazing at it initially through a car window and tramping to it through a car-park. Follow the track downhill towards the castle, going over a stile next to a metal gate and through an ungated wall. Pass below the castle and turn RIGHT when you meet a track coming from the left.

2 The entrance to the castle is now immediately on the RIGHT. To buy entrance tickets (and continue the walk) follow the now surfaced road downhill a short distance before going RIGHT onto a path and down steps which take you to a metal gate on the RIGHT. Go through the gate, turn LEFT and then RIGHT to reach the castle ticket office. *When this is closed tickets are available at the farmhouse next door. They cost £2 or £1.50 for over-60s and children. The castle is open daily except over Christmas and New Year. Dolwyddelan Castle was built early in the 13th Century although the now ruinous West Tower was added later, probably by Edward 1. Maredudd ap Ieuan ap Robert, of the Wynn Family of Gwydir, subsequently lived in the castle and built Dowyddelan Church. He also owned a house in the Penamnen Valley (see* **Walk 8***) above the village.*

3 From the ticket office go downhill towards the main A470 road. On the way you will pass a pe-fabricated, black-painted barn. Turn RIGHT just beyond this and go through a metal gate (or over the stile next to it) and follow the track across a field to another metal gate and stile. Go through/over and continue through another gateway (with adjoining stile), ignoring a track with a gate leading left into the castle car-park and bearing RIGHT uphill to a marker. Pass this to reach another metal gate and stile. *From here you get a good view of the flooded mine workings below you to the left. There are several such workings near Dolwyddelan although none were really successful.* Continue ahead across a field making for a marker above you and half-RIGHT. Pass

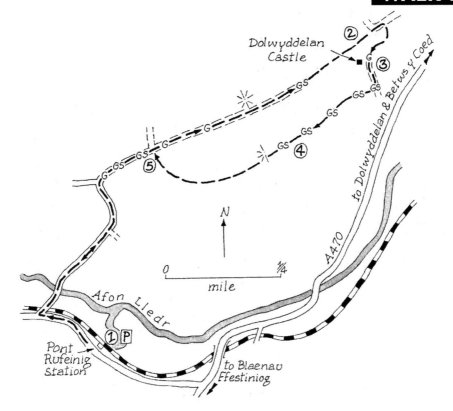

Dolwyddelan
Castle

to Dolwyddelan & Betws y Coed

N

A470

0   ¼   mile

Afon Lledr

Pont
Rufeinig
Station

to Blaenau
Ffestiniog

this and continue half-RIGHT to a stile next to two metal gates.

4 Cross the stile and then go LEFT, walking next to the fence on your left. *There's a good view from here of the Crimea Pass over which the A470 goes to Blaenau Ffestiniog.* Soon the path ascends gently to another marker from where you should continue along the fence to a marker which points RIGHT uphill. Scramble up to another marker and bear LEFT to follow the path along the edge of a rocky knoll and then RIGHT alongside a fence to a metal gate with marker. Go through and you are back on the original track. *Note the spectacular views ahead, notably of the Snowdon range.*

5 Follow the track through a series of metal gates to reach a metalled road amidst farm buildings. Go LEFT onto the road and follow it back to Roman Bridge station.

Dolwyddelan Castle

WALK 17
BLAENAU DOLWYDDELAN

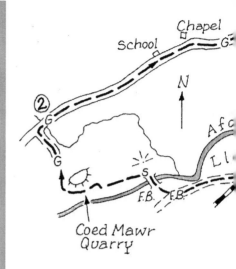

DESCRIPTION A walk which explores the settlement above Dolwyddelan in the Lledr Valley. The 4½-mile circuit takes you from the railway halt at Roman Bridge across the Afon Lledr and past a school and chapel, now converted into dwellings, and quarry-workings, which, a hundred years ago, were the focus of a once busy way of life in this beautiful valley. Allow 2 hours.

START Parking space at Pont Rufeinig (Roman Bridge) station (SH713514).

DIRECTIONS *From Betws-y-Coed:* From its junction with the A5 just south of Betws-y-Coed take the A470 towards Blaenau Ffestiniog. Pass through Dolwyddelan and, about a mile beyond the village, take the minor road on the RIGHT signposted Roman Bridge station. Park by the station on the RIGHT. *From Blaenau Ffestiniog:* Take the A470 north in the direction of Conwy. The road climbs over the Crimea Pass and descends steeply into the Lledr Valley. Near the bottom of the descent, soon after a three-lane stretch of road, take the minor road on the LEFT signposted Roman Bridge station. Park by the station on the RIGHT.

I Follow the road RIGHT to a junction. Go LEFT here to a farmhouse, through a gateway and turn RIGHT. *The farmhouse is named Gorddinan. The nearby pass over the mountains to Blaenau Ffestiniog originally shared the same name, for the top of the pass is the watershed for the Afon Gorddinan which flows down to join the Afon Lledr near the farmhouse. The pass has since become called the Crimea Pass, apparently because soldiers returning from the Crimean War likened the pass under snow to regions of the Crimea where they had fought.* Go through a metal gate, then RIGHT through another metal gate and over a railway bridge. Go LEFT to a bridge over a stream and then sharp LEFT. Here go RIGHT off the track to cross a stream and a stile. *There is a good*

view of Moel Siabod to the right from here. Cross the River Lledr on a wooden bridge. Then turn sharp LEFT, walking towards two marker posts. Turn RIGHT by the second, going uphill, and then LEFT at the fence. *The fence surrounds the workings of Coed Mawr quarry which was opened in about 1870. The remains of the quarry's engine-house can be seen.* Follow the fence RIGHT (look for the marker), then go RIGHT around the end of the quarry workings, making for a track and metal gate. Follow the track to a tarmac road. *Facing you on the left across the road are the ruins of what appears once to have been quite a substantial chapel, possibly used by workers at the two nearby quarries (see* **Walk 18)**.

2 Turn RIGHT onto the road, and follow it across a stream, through a metal gate and along the valley. *As you walk you will pass the converted school building and chapel, on the left, which once played a significant part in the life of this remote valley.* Soon, pass through another metal gate, usually open, and then below a large white house up to the left. Just after this turn RIGHT at a footpath sign. Follow the marked path to a metal gate. Go ahead, then RIGHT to a wooden gate and footbridge. Cross a field and bear RIGHT to a ramp to a wooden gate and road.

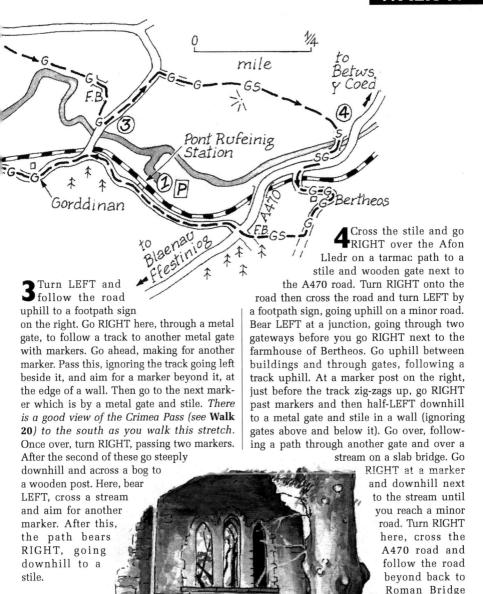

0   ¼

mile

to Betws y Coed

G
F.B.
G
G — G — GS
G
③
Pont Rufeinig Station
④
S
SG
G — G
G — G
Bertheos
G — G
⚲
Gorddinan
⚲ P ②
to Blaenau Ffestiniog
F.B. GS
A470

3 Turn LEFT and follow the road uphill to a footpath sign on the right. Go RIGHT here, through a metal gate, to follow a track to another metal gate with markers. Go ahead, making for another marker. Pass this, ignoring the track going left beside it, and aim for a marker beyond it, at the edge of a wall. Then go to the next marker which is by a metal gate and stile. *There is a good view of the Crimea Pass (see* **Walk 20***) to the south as you walk this stretch.* Once over, turn RIGHT, passing two markers. After the second of these go steeply downhill and across a bog to a wooden post. Here, bear LEFT, cross a stream and aim for another marker. After this, the path bears RIGHT, going downhill to a stile.

4 Cross the stile and go RIGHT over the Afon Lledr on a tarmac path to a stile and wooden gate next to the A470 road. Turn RIGHT onto the road then cross the road and turn LEFT by a footpath sign, going uphill on a minor road. Bear LEFT at a junction, going through two gateways before you go RIGHT next to the farmhouse of Bertheos. Go uphill between buildings and through gates, following a track uphill. At a marker post on the right, just before the track zig-zags up, go RIGHT past markers and then half-LEFT downhill to a metal gate and stile in a wall (ignoring gates above and below it). Go over, following a path through another gate and over a stream on a slab bridge. Go RIGHT at a marker and downhill next to the stream until you reach a minor road. Turn RIGHT here, cross the A470 road and follow the road beyond back to Roman Bridge station.

Ruins near Coed Mawr Quarry

COED MAWR

DESCRIPTION This fascinating 2½-mile walk takes you to four sites which, a hundred years ago, dominated life in the upper Lledr Valley: the slate quarries of Hendre and Coed Mawr, and the farming settlements which share their names. The walk takes you across the Afon Lledr twice, once on a footbridge and the second time on stepping stones placed to facilitate contact between the inhabitants of the two remote farms on opposite sides of the valley. Allow 1½ hours. Please note that the second river crossing becomes impassable when the Lledr is in spate.

START Parking space at the end of the road which leads past Pont Rufeinig (Roman Bridge) station to the head of the Lledr Valley (SH696513).

DIRECTIONS *From Betws-y-Coed:* From its junction with the A5 just south of Betws-y-Coed take the A470 towards Blaenau Ffestiniog. Pass through Dolwyddelan and, about a mile beyond the village, take the minor road on the RIGHT signposted Roman Bridge station. Follow the tarmac road, ignoring any turns off it, to its end (about 2 miles) and park in the space on the RIGHT. *From Blaenau Ffestiniog:* Take the A470 north in the direction of Conwy. The road climbs over the Crimea Pass and descends steeply into the Lledr Valley. Near the bottom of the descent, soon after a three-lane stretch of road, take the minor road on the LEFT signposted Roman Bridge station. Follow the tarmac road, ignoring any turns off it, to its end (about 2 miles) and park in the space on the RIGHT.

I Follow the track which leads away from the parking space and crosses a bridge before going uphill. Just over the bridge turn LEFT through a metal gate and over a stile next to a wooden gate. Follow a track through mine workings making for a white footpath sign. *This is Hendre quarry, which opened in about 1840 and was worked for some 60 years. Water-power was used for haulage and the slate produced in the quarry was unusually black in shade.* Go downhill

on a faint path on the right from this point to reach the flooded pit of the quarry. *This is an eerily atmospheric place with steep cliffs and lush foliage surrounding the deep water.* Return to the main track and turn RIGHT, following it past spoil-heaps to another footpath sign. Soon you reach a marker pointing RIGHT to a wooden gate with a 'freedom to roam' sign on it. Go through, downhill past another marker and then out of the quarry workings. The path continues past markers with a fence and the Afon Lledr on the left. It then bears half-RIGHT uphill between trees onto a rocky knoll. (If you miss this turn you will come to a fence barring your way. If so retrace your steps.) You then come to a fence at right-angles and a sign pointing RIGHT. Then go LEFT over a stile with a yellow marker on it. Walk ahead parallel with a fence and the river on your left. Soon go LEFT over a stile and then cross the Lledr on a wooden bridge.

2 Then turn sharp LEFT, walking towards two marker posts. Turn RIGHT by the second, going uphill, and then LEFT at the fence. *The fence surrounds the workings of Coed Mawr quarry which was opened in about 1870. The remains of the quarry's engine-house can be seen. Slate from the workings was transported down the Lledr Valley on carts.* Follow the fence RIGHT (look for the marker), then go LEFT, making for a house. Go through a metal gate, cross a bridge and reach a road. Turn LEFT and immediately take the RIGHT fork, signposted Coed Mawr.

3 The farm road goes steeply uphill. At the farm, go through a metal gate. *After closing this take a moment to look back down the valley with Dolwyddelam nestling below its twin mountains of Moel Siabod to the left and Ro Wen to the right.* Walk past a green corrugated barn, turn LEFT immediately after it and then go between buildings to a metal gate. Once through go half-RIGHT, walking downhill between bushes and trees, and then through a gap in a low wall. Make for a stile ahead, go over, and then cross the Lledr on the stepping stones beyond. Go across a rough, boggy field, mak-

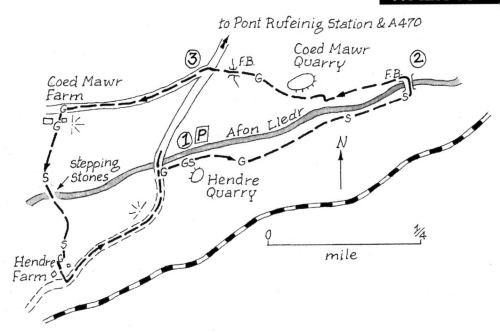

to Pont Rufeinig Station & A470

ing for another stile below the outbuildings of Hendre Farm which you can see ahead. Go uphill, once over the stile, walking towards an electricity pole next to which you should bear RIGHT onto a track going up to a large barn. Turn LEFT here, go through a gate and bear LEFT up between farm buildings. When you reach a track coming from Hendre farmhouse on the right go LEFT onto it and follow it uphill. The track then descends to the bridge next to Hendre quarry. *There is a good view of the ridge of Y Cribau (see* **Walk 15***) as you begin the descent.* Once over the bridge you are back where you started.

Hendre Quarry

UNDER MOEL DYRNOGYDD

DESCRIPTION This interesting walk takes you on an old mine track from the shelter of the Lledr Valley to the exposed moorland under Moel Dyrnogydd (see **Walk 20**) where, a century ago, slate was quarried in a constant battle with the elements. The track climbs above the entrance to the long railway tunnel between Roman Bridge and Blaenau Ffestiniog which passes below the mine workings. The tunnel is marked by a ventilation shaft amidst the mine workings. Allow 2 hours for this 4-mile walk.

START Parking space at the end of the road which leads past Pont Rufeinig (Roman Bridge) station to the head of the Lledr Valley (SH696513).

DIRECTIONS *From Betws-y-Coed:* From its junction with the A5 just south of Betws-y-Coed take the A470 towards Blaenau Ffestiniog. Pass through Dolwyddelan and, about a mile beyond the village, take the minor road on the RIGHT signposted Roman Bridge station. Follow the tarmac road, ignoring any turns off it, to its end (about 2 miles) and park in the space on the RIGHT. *From Blaenau Ffestiniog:* Take the A470 north in the direction of Conwy. The road climbs over the Crimea Pass and descends steeply into the Lledr Valley. Near the bottom of the descent, soon after a three-lane stretch of road, take the minor road on the LEFT signposted Roman Bridge station. Follow the tarmac road, ignoring any turns off it, to its end (about 2 miles) and park in the space on the RIGHT.

I Follow the track which leads away from the parking space and crosses a bridge before going uphill. Ignore left and right turns just after the bridge and pass a sign for 'Hendre' as you climb. Soon the railway line comes into view over to the left and the track descends to pass the farm of Hendre. Go through a metal gate and ignore a right turn just before the farmhouse. Pass the house and go uphill through a second gate. The track continues uphill and, at the point when it bears right and descends towards a high stone wall go gently LEFT uphill on a faint track alongside a stone-built embankment. Then go LEFT under a railway bridge and through a wooden gate. Follow the track uphill alongside a fence on the left. The track then twists and turns downhill and crosses a stream. Soon you reach a stile and wooden gate through a wall which comes up from the right. *At this point you are above the cutting and entrance to the 3.4km long railway tunnel to Blaenau Ffestiniog. The railway line was opened in 1879 and the fact that it survives today is something of a miracle. There are six or so passenger trains between Blaenau and Llandudno in each direction on weekdays and there are plans for the line to be used by trains carrying slate down to the coast.* Soon you come to the remains of a large ruined settlement across the river on the right. *There is an attractive bridge to the settlement. This is a beautiful spot and dramatic in terms of waterfalls and rapids when the Afon Lledr is in spate. The largest of the ruined buildings has the appearance of a chapel and the settlement will have been of some importance in the days when the track was in use as a mine access and short-cut from the top of the Crimea Pass (see **Walk 20**) to upper Dolwyddelan.*

2 The track is well engineered and leads gently uphill away from the settlement and through a wall, using a series of zig-zags to gain height before levelling off. A line of electricity poles comes into view. *These pass the end of Llyn Dyrnogydd (see **Walk 20**) and cross the shoulder of Moel Dyrnogydd which dominates the near skyline from now on.* Soon you reach a metal gate with a stile to its left. *Stop at this point to admire the view back over the Lledr Valley to the twin summits of Cribau (see **Walk 15**), the Glyder range and the summit of Moel Siabod (see **Walk 7**).* The track turns RIGHT and, after a short distance you come to the entrance to the quarry workings on the right. Go RIGHT uphill here to arrive at a series of ten narrow spoil ramps. *From here there is a magnificent view north and west. The Carneddau can be see over the shoulder of Moel Siabod and the ridge stretching from Ysgafell Wen* to Yr Arddu forms the skyline to the west. Around you are the remains of several substantial quarry buildings, one of which is paved inside. Just above the buildings is a ventilation shaft, built to allow the escape of smoke and fumes from the railway tunnel below. Sections of light railway line can be found amongst the quarry workings, suggesting that tracks were originally laid along the spoil ramps to allow spoil to be moved by truck.

3 Return to the main track and turn LEFT. Retrace your steps by following the track back to the parking space in the Lledr Valley.

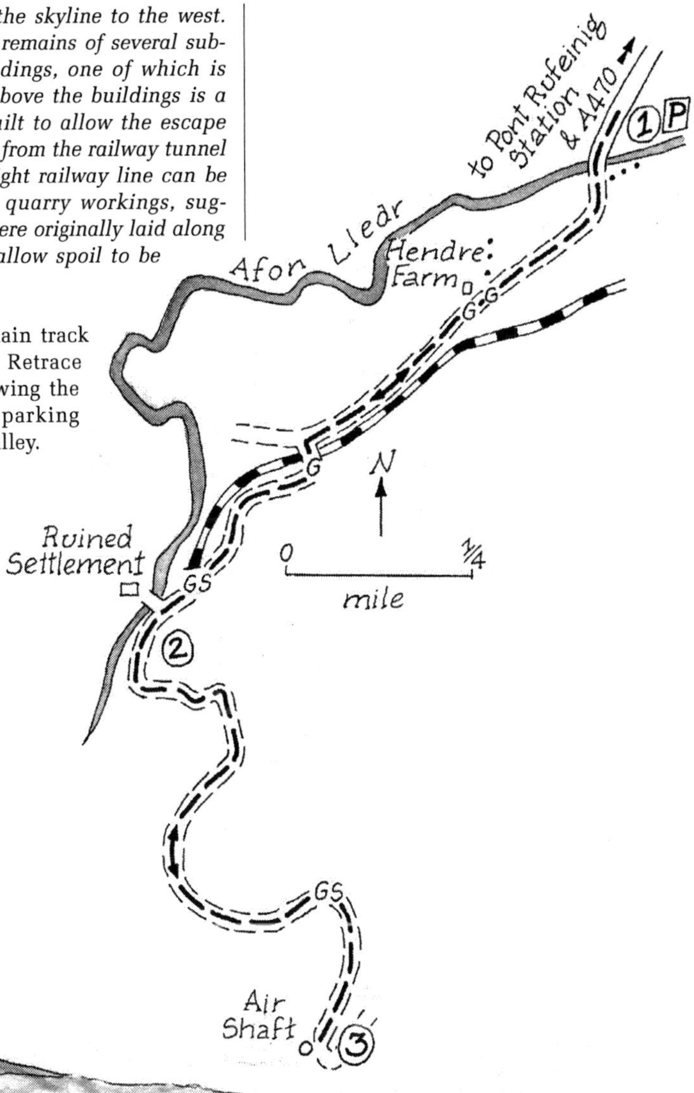

to Pont Rufeinig Station & A470

① P

Afon Lledr

Hendre Farm

Ruined Settlement

GS

N

0   ¼

mile

②

GS

Air Shaft ③

Quarry workings below Moel Dyrnogydd, showing the air shaft from the railway tunnel

MOEL DYRNOGYDD FROM THE CRIMEA PASS

DESCRIPTION A 2½-mile walk which provides magnificent views for comparatively little effort. You begin by following a well-made track which leads from the top of the Crimea Pass to the remains of Bwlch Gorddinan quarry. From here it is a short climb to the top of Moel Dyrnogydd which, because of its pointed summit and isolated position, gives a wide-ranging panorama. The return journey takes you down past the well-hidden Llyn Dyrnogydd to re-join the mine track. Allow 2½ hours.

START Parking area on the A470 just north of the top of the Crimea Pass (SH702488).

DIRECTIONS *From Betws-y-Coed:* From its junction with the A5 just south of Betws-y-Coed take the A470 towards Blaenau Ffestiniog. Pass through Dolwyddelan and follow the road as it climbs steeply uphill after the junction with a minor road on the right which is signposted to Roman Bridge station. After about two miles you will see a parking area, with trees, on the left. Park here. *From Blaenau Ffestiniog:* Take the A470 north in the direction of Conwy. This climbs steeply to the top of the Crimea Pass and, soon after the road begins to descend, you will see a parking area, with trees, on the RIGHT. Park here.

1 Cross the road and turn LEFT, following it uphill towards the top of the pass. After a short distance you will come to a stile next to a gate on the RIGHT. Cross this and follow the track beyond which leads initially west towards Moel Dyrnogydd, the mountain ahead of you. The well-made track bears RIGHT around the side of Moel Dyrnogydd and then goes LEFT. *There is a particularly good view northwards of Moel Siabod (see* **Walk 7***) and of the upper Lledr Valley from this point.* Soon the working of Bwlch Gorddinan quarry come into sight on the left and the track passes between two massive boulders to reach a metal gate and stile. *Bwlch Gorddinan is the original name for the Crimea Pass. The top of the pass is the watershed for the Afon Gorddinan which flows down to join the Afon Lledr near a farmhouse named Gorddinan. There are workings to left and right of the track before the gate and the incline used for lowering trucks full of waste is a conspicuous feature of the quarry remains on the hillside above you.* Go over the stile and continue walking until you near a second metal gate.

2 Turn LEFT a short distance before the gate, next to a spoil heap and wall of rock on the right. Walk up the hillside, keeping initially to the right of the main quarry workings and left of a rocky outcrop, making for a gully above you. Go into the gully, climbing up it until you reach a fence. Bear LEFT at the fence and, keeping to the left of this, follow it uphill to the summit of Moel Dyrnogydd. *The view from this isolated peak is superlative. To the south you can see Allt Fawr above Blaenau Ffestiniog and, in the distance, Rhobell Fawr, the Rhinog range and Cadair Idris. To the north-west are the Snowdon and Glyder ranges, and Moel Siabod which towers above Dolwyddelan and its castle. The other mountain which is associated with Dolwyddelan, Ro Wen (see* **Walk 13***), can be seen to the east and, northwards, the Conwy Valley leads the eye to the north coast of Wales.*

3 Leave the summit by following the fence in the opposite direction to that from which arrived, keeping to the left of it. Ahead of you is Allt Fawr and as you begin to descend you will see Llyn Dyrnogydd suddenly appear below. When the fence begins to climb out of a dip in the hillside just above the end of the lake, turn sharp LEFT and go down towards the lake alongside a rocky and heather-covered slope on your right. Pass through the remains of a wall as you descend and bear gently RIGHT to reach the end of the lake. *At just over 1400 ft, Llyn Dyrnogydd is in a remote and peaceful spot. It is 4½ acres in area and was once famous for the size of its trout.*

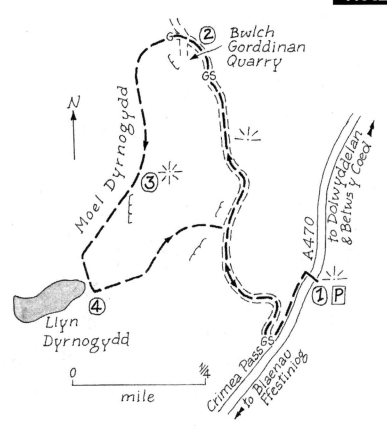

4 Leave the lake by walking up the gently sloping gully which leads away eastwards from its end. Keep to the left of the gully, below a rocky outcrop, and bear slightly LEFT at its upper end when the main A470 road comes into sight ahead and below. Make directly for the road, traversing another gully, before going half-RIGHT downhill. Keep to the LEFT of the stream as you head towards the trees and car-park on the road. As you near the bottom of the stream gully bear gently LEFT to avoid a steep, rocky section of hillside and then continue to make for the car-park. Soon,

when the mine track comes into view, wind your way down the grassy hillside to join it, turning RIGHT. Follow the track to the main road, cross over the stile and turn LEFT to follow the A470 back to the parking area.

Moel Dyrnogydd from the north

PRONUNCIATION

These basic points should help non-Welsh speakers

Welsh	English equivalent
c	always hard, as in cat
ch	as in the Scottish word loch
dd	as 'th' in then
f	as 'f' in of
ff	as 'ff' in off
g	always hard as in got
ll	no real equivalent. It is like 'th' in then, but with an 'L' sound added to it, giving 'thlan' for the pronunciation of the Welsh Llan.

In Welsh the accent usually falls on the last-but-one syllable of a word.

KEY TO THE MAPS

- ➡ Walk route & direction
- — Main road
- --- Minor road
- .... Adjoining path
- ∿ River or stream
- ♣ ♤ Woods or forest
- ▬ Railway
- **G** Gate
- **S** Stile
- ☼ Viewpoint
- P Parking
- T Telephone

THE COUNTRYSIDE CODE

- Be safe – plan ahead and follow any signs

- Leave gates and property as you find them

- Protect plants and animals, and take your litter home

- Keep dogs under close control

- Consider other people

Published by
Kittiwake
3 Glantwymyn Village Workshops, Glantwymyn, Machynlleth, Montgomeryshire SY20 8LY

© Text: Michael Burnett 2006
© Maps & illustrations: Kittiwake 2006

Drawings by Morag Perrott

Cover photographs of Dolwyddelan: David Perrott

Care has been taken to be accurate.
However neither the author nor the publisher can accept responsibility for any errors which may appear, or their consequences. If you are in any doubt about access, always check before you proceed.

Printed by MWL, Pontypool..

ISBN: **978 1 902302 40 9**